Spelling
Skills

AGE 8-9

Exercises devised by Nicola Morgan MA
an experienced teacher and educational consultant
Illustrated by Pip Adams

Spelling Skills 8-9 forms part of **Learning Rewards**, a home-learning programme designed to help your child succeed at school with the National Curriculum. It has been extensively researched with children and teachers.

This book stands alone as a support for spelling for this age group, but is also a natural follow-on to *Spelling Skills 7-8*. The companion titles, *Reading Skills* and *Writing Skills* complete the programme for Key Stage 2 language.

Good spelling depends on several skills: listening, looking, remembering and practising. All these skills are developed in this book, through structured and enjoyable activities. It is useful to buy or make a small notebook for your child to write the words he or she learns. Use one page of the notebook for each letter of the alphabet.

Encourage your child to use the Spelling Code:

1. LOOK at a word carefully
2. SAY the letters
3. COVER the word
4. WRITE the word
5. CHECK the spelling

The level of the spelling exercises is progressive in this book, so try to work through them in order. It is important to stop before your child has had enough and to return at a later date to any exercise that he or she is struggling with.

The fold-out progress chart is a useful record of your child's performance and helps identify his or her strengths and weaknesses. Always reward your child's work with lots of encouragement and a gold star.

When you come to the end of the book, you will find a fun, wipe-clean learning game.

Key to symbols on the page:

 skills covered by each exercise as they relate to the National Curriculum

 notes for parents, explaining specific teaching points

 follow-up activities which will extend your child's understanding of the exercise

commissioning editor: Nina Filipek series editor: Stephanie Sloan
designer: Gail Rose cover design: Paul Dronsfield

Published in Great Britain by
World International Limited, Deanway Technology Centre,
Wilmslow Road, Handforth, Cheshire SK9 3FB.
Printed in Italy.
ISBN 0 7498 4018 8

How we learn to spell

To learn different ways of spelling words.

Some words have the same letter patterns, so you can learn them in groups. Sort the words below into two groups.

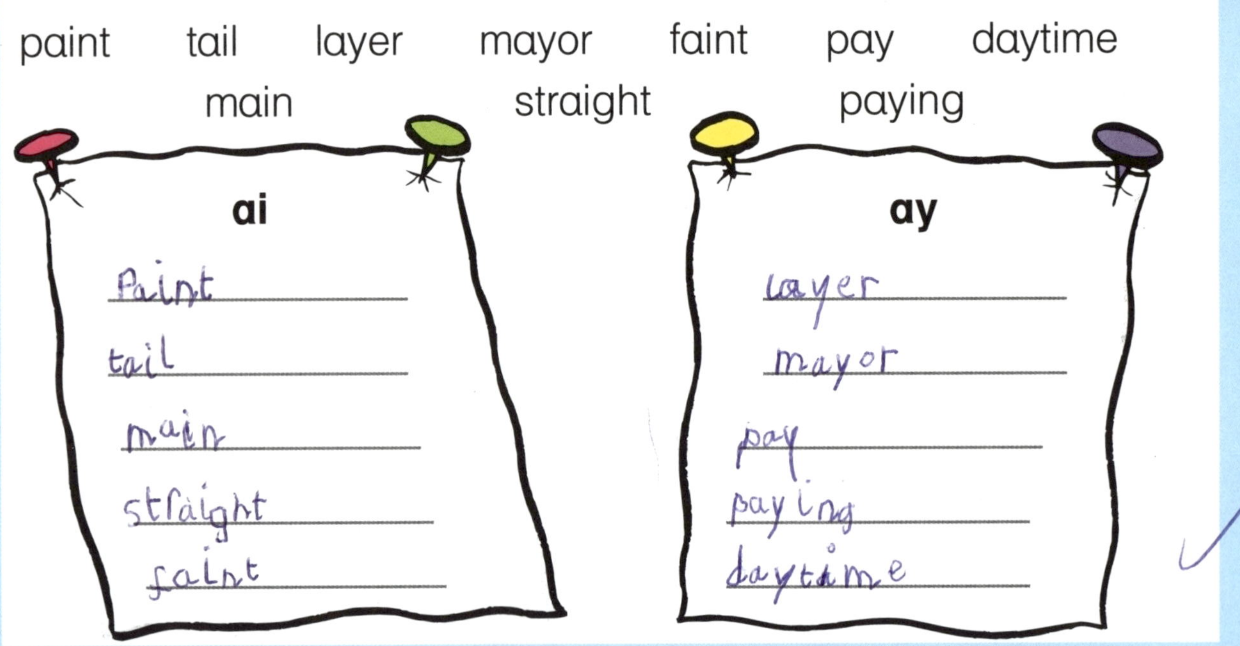

When you learn a word, you should:

LOOK at it	SAY the letters	COVER it	WRITE it	CHECK it

Practise the LOOK SAY method using these words:

enough **double**

LOOK SAY COVER WRITE ______________ CHECK

LOOK SAY COVER WRITE ______________ CHECK

If you don't know the spelling of a word, guess how it starts and use a dictionary. There's one on page 32 which you'll need for the work in this book.

It's important that spellings are learnt gradually and systematically. Concentrate particularly on words your child will actually use.

To learn the difference between short and long vowel sounds.

Same letter, different sound

Vowels (a, e, i, o, u) can make **short** sounds, as in **ant** and **egg**, or **long** sounds, as in **ape** and **soap**. When two vowels go together, they make a long sound.

Listen to the **short** vowels in these words:

catch

lunch

sit

Listen to the **long** vowels in these words:

blue

peach

cake

Sort these words into long and short vowels.
Remember to LOOK and SAY.

long		short
spear	spear	pet
joke	brush	brush
smile	joke	wish
take	smile	man
	wish	
	pet	
	take	
	man	

Spelling with **tch** and **ch**

To learn to spell words with **tch** and **ch**.

After a short vowel, write **tch**. After anything else, write **ch**.

tch	**ch**
fetch	beach
pitch	coach
watch	torch

These words are different. You need to learn them.

The **rich** man wore a coat
which was covered in **such**
a lot of gold that it looked
much too heavy to wear.

Fill in the spaces using the words at the bottom of the page. Use each word once.

Go and f e t c h a basket to put our picnic l u n c h in.

You must check e a c h word carefully.

I have s u c h a sore back that I can't t o u c h my toes.

Buy or make a notebook for your child to write useful spellings in.

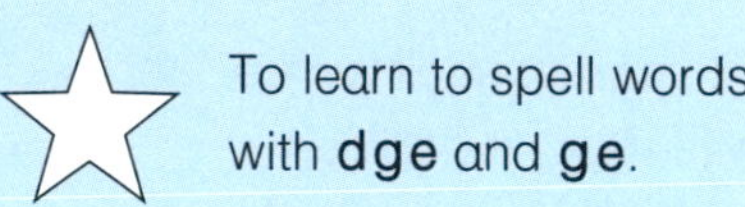

To learn to spell words with **dge** and **ge**.

Spelling with **dge** and **ge**

After a short vowel, write **dge**. After anything else, write **ge**.

dge	**ge**
badger	page
fudge	age
hedge	huge

Can you finish this puzzle?

Across

1. like toffee, but softer
4. enormous
5. something inside a book
7. a boat on a canal
9. a very tiny push
10. someone who makes a fake

Down

2. must be done immediately
3. bigger
4. divides one garden from another
6. a very long time
8. the side of something

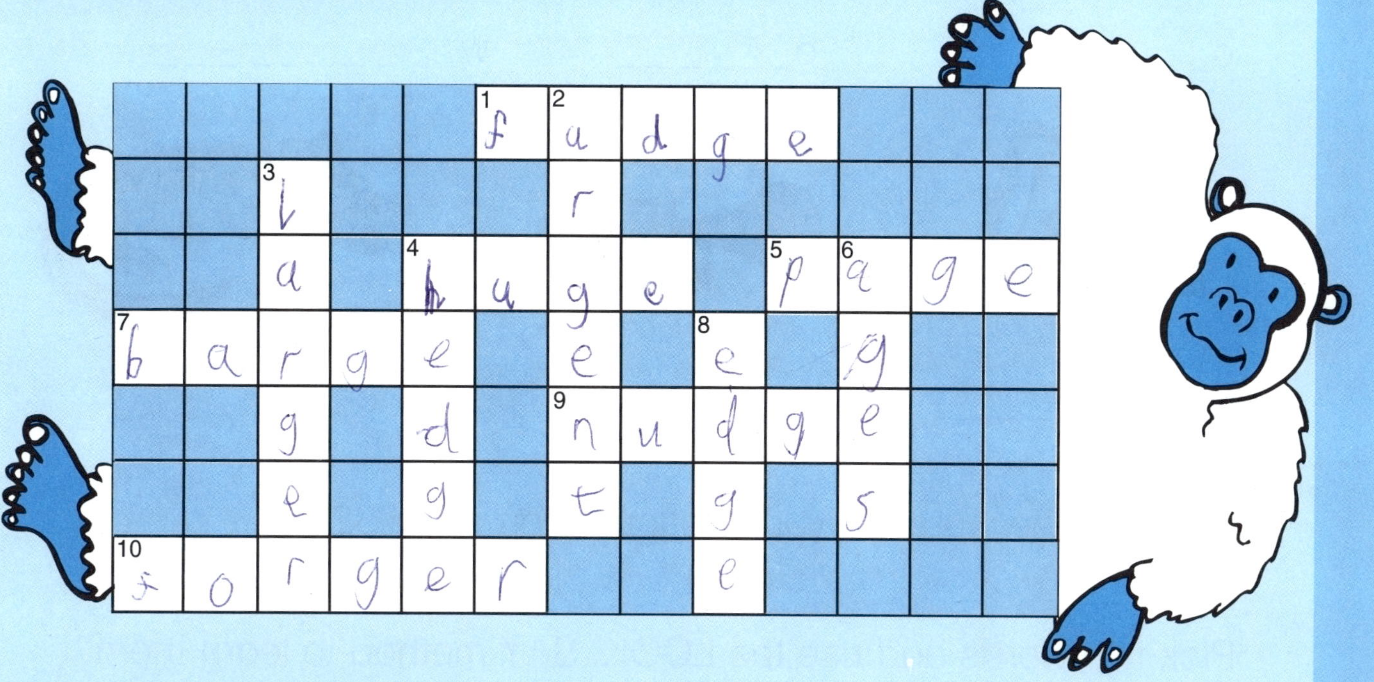

Encourage your child to do puzzles. These are a good way to have fun while learning new meanings and spellings.

Syllables

To learn to spell words with many syllables.

Words are easier to spell if you break them into syllables.

Split these words into syllables.

calendar   animal   thunder   anybody

cal/en/dar   ______   ________   ________

p________   a________   r______

c______   b______   w___________

p__________   t______   c________

Check all the words in your dictionary on page 32.

Pick two words and use the LOOK, SAY method to learn them.

LOOK   SAY   COVER   WRITE ____________ CHECK

LOOK   SAY   COVER   WRITE ____________ CHECK

To learn to spell more words with many syllables.

Syllables

Spell these words by splitting them into syllables.

u_ _ _ _ _ _ _

o_ _ _ _ _ _

s_ _ _ _ _ _ _ _ _

f_ _ _ _ _ – _ _ _

p_ _ _ _ _ – _ _ _ _

r_ _ _ _ _ _ _

Make some long words using one syllable from each list. The first one has been done for you.

im	norm	or	________
ex	mor	cise	________
e	spect	row	________
to	port	ous	________
in	er	ant	________

Which word do you most want to know how to spell?

LOOK SAY COVER WRITE ________ CHECK

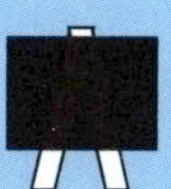

Although there are rules about where words break into syllables, it doesn't matter at this stage. Let your child break words where it seems most natural to do so.

Adding to the start of words

To learn to spell words with prefixes.

Prefixes are bits we add to the beginning of words.
Each prefix has a meaning.

tele means 'from a distance'
telephone, telegram, telegraph

mis means 'wrong'
mistake, misspell, misdirect

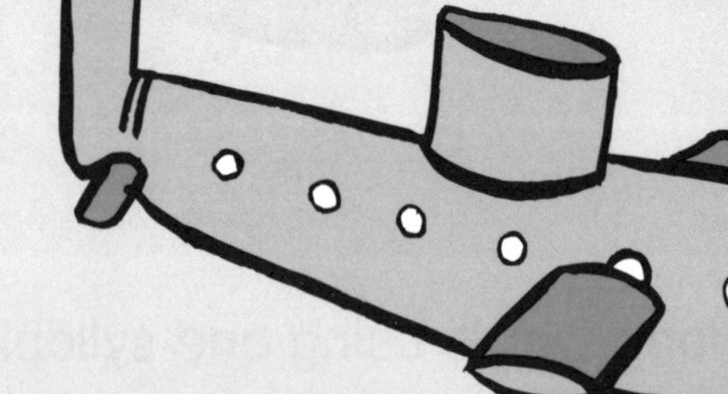

sub means 'under'
submarine, subway

Join each prefix to the right word. Guess what each whole word means, then ask a grown-up if you are right.

tele ____________ mis ____________ sub ____________

tele ____________ mis ____________ sub ____________

understand **phone** **soil** **read** **merge** **scope**

Do you know any other **tele**, **mis** or **sub** words?

These are difficult words, but it is important for children to begin developing a wide vocabulary, even at the risk of some incorrect spellings.

To learn to spell words with suffixes.

Adding to the end of words

Suffixes are bits we add to the end of words.

Drop the **e** if you add an ending that starts with a vowel:
hope+ing = hoping   shake+er = shaker

When the word ends in **y**, change it to an **i**.
happy+er = happier   silly+ness = silliness

But, when the suffix starts with **i**, then leave the **y**:
carry+ing = carrying

Following these rules, fill in the gaps in the table:

	-ing	-ed	-ly	ness
hope				
happy				
love				
marry				
use				

Choose four of the words you have just made. Make a funny sentence using all of them. Then illustrate it.

The root word

To learn what word roots are.

The root is the word we start with before we add prefixes and suffixes.
The root of 'unhappiness' is 'happy' – this is the word we start with before we add **un** and **ness** to it.

Take away any prefixes and suffixes to find the root of these words.

~~un~~comfort~~able~~	television	hopeless
_ _ _ _ _ _ _	_ _ _ _ _ _	_ _ _ _
usefulness	mishandled	teleprompter
_ _ _ _ _ _	_ _ _ _ _ _	_ _ _ _ _ _

The newsreader forgot to wear her glasses and she could not read the teleprompter.

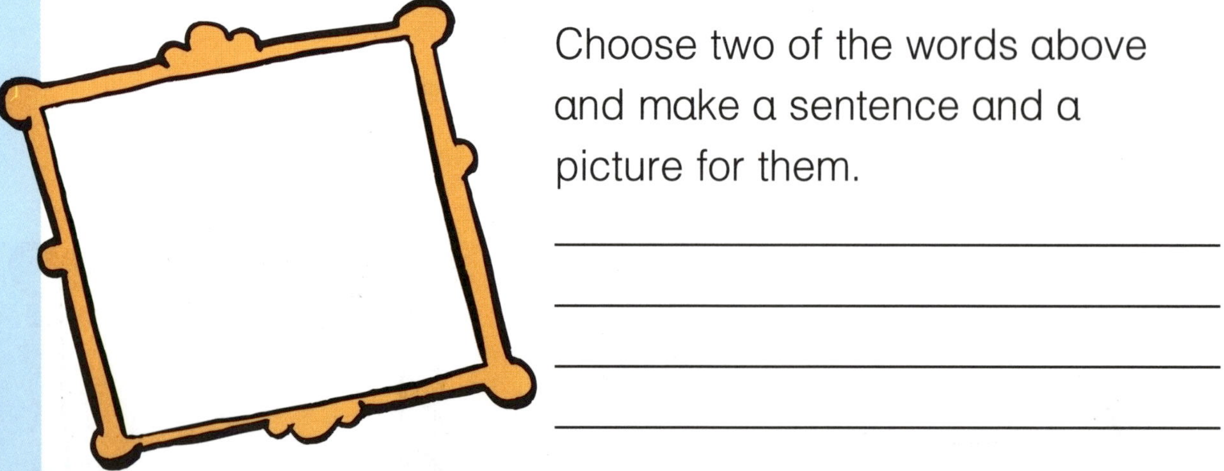

Choose two of the words above and make a sentence and a picture for them.

____

____

____

____

Breaking words into roots, prefixes and suffixes develops vocabulary as well as spelling. Soon your child will begin to see that there are patterns to words.

The letter **w** – rules

To learn how the letter **w** changes **o** and **a** sounds.

w makes 'a' sound like 'o':

want watch wander wand wasp swap

w makes 'o' sound like 'u':

won wonderful worry

w makes 'ar' sound like 'or':

ward warning war warrior

w makes 'or' sounds like 'ur':

word worm worse work

And sometimes w does nothing strange at all:

wag waggle swore worn (out)

Can you finish this puzzle? The answers all contain **w**.

Across

1. the opposite of peace
3. insects which sting
5. a fierce fighter
6. things you say and write
8. brilliant, amazing

Down

1. wriggly creature in the garden
2. where you stay in a hospital
4. promised very strongly
6. a magician uses it
7. frozen rain

Puzzle practice

To practise what has been learnt so far.

These puzzles are to practise all you have learnt so far.

Each word on the wheel ends with the first letter of the following word.

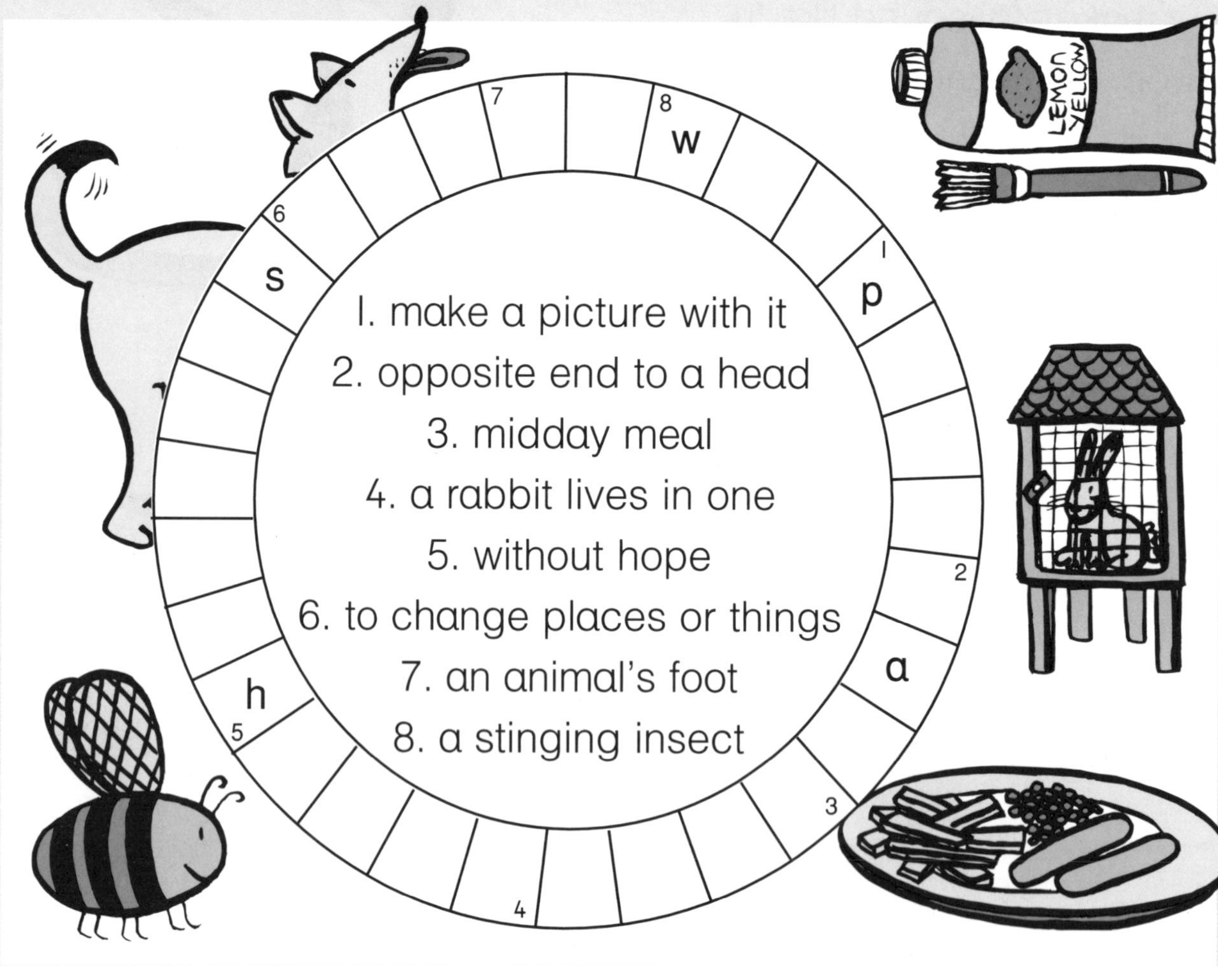

1. make a picture with it
2. opposite end to a head
3. midday meal
4. a rabbit lives in one
5. without hope
6. to change places or things
7. an animal's foot
8. a stinging insect

Think of your own words to fill in these steps. Make the last letter of each word the first letter of the next.

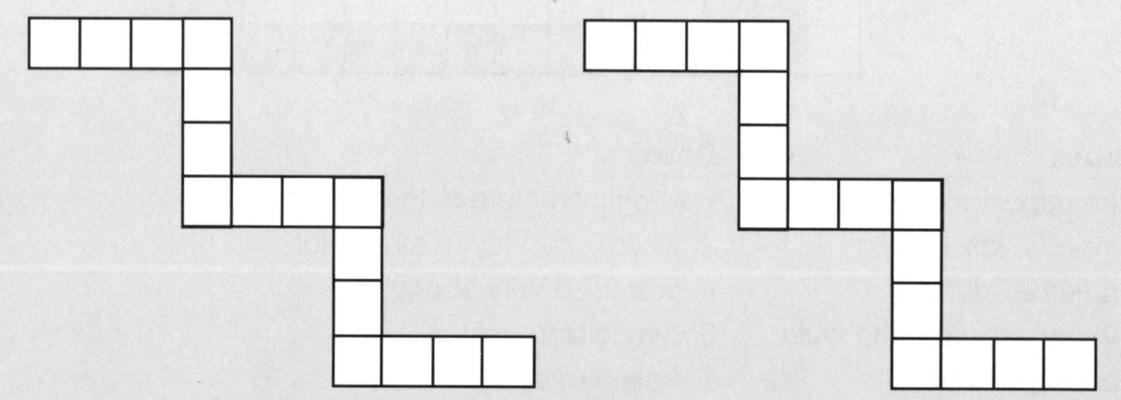

To practise what has been learnt so far.

Puzzle practice

Make words using one syllable from each list.

re	ma	en	
ca	tak	pus	
sub	cord	van	
oc	ing–	er	
mis	ra	pan	
fry	to	rine	

Can you spell these things?

t_ _ _ _ _ _ _ _ c_ _ _ _ _ _ _ r_ _ _ _ _ _ _

c_ _ _ _ _ _ _ _ p_ _ _ _ _ _ _ _ _ s_ _ _e_ _ _ _

Remind your child to add any useful words to his or her notebook.

Long **o** sound

To learn the different ways of writing the long **o** sound.

There are lots of ways of writing the long **o** sound, as you hear in 'Oh, no!'

Listen to the sounds of the words. Draw lines from each one to the correct bowl.

float alone throw old pole don't

low roast joke snow gold soak

Can you spell these words?

_ _ _ _

_ _ _ _ _

_ _ _ _

Check the words in the dictionary on page 32.

It's important for your child to practise checking spellings in a dictionary. To build his or her confidence, make sure you use a dictionary which is not too complicated.

To learn the different ways of writing the long **i** sound.

Long i sound

There are lots of ways of writing the long i sound, as in 'Hi!'

Write each of these words on the correct kite.

light	kite	tried	my
hide	night	tyre	tie

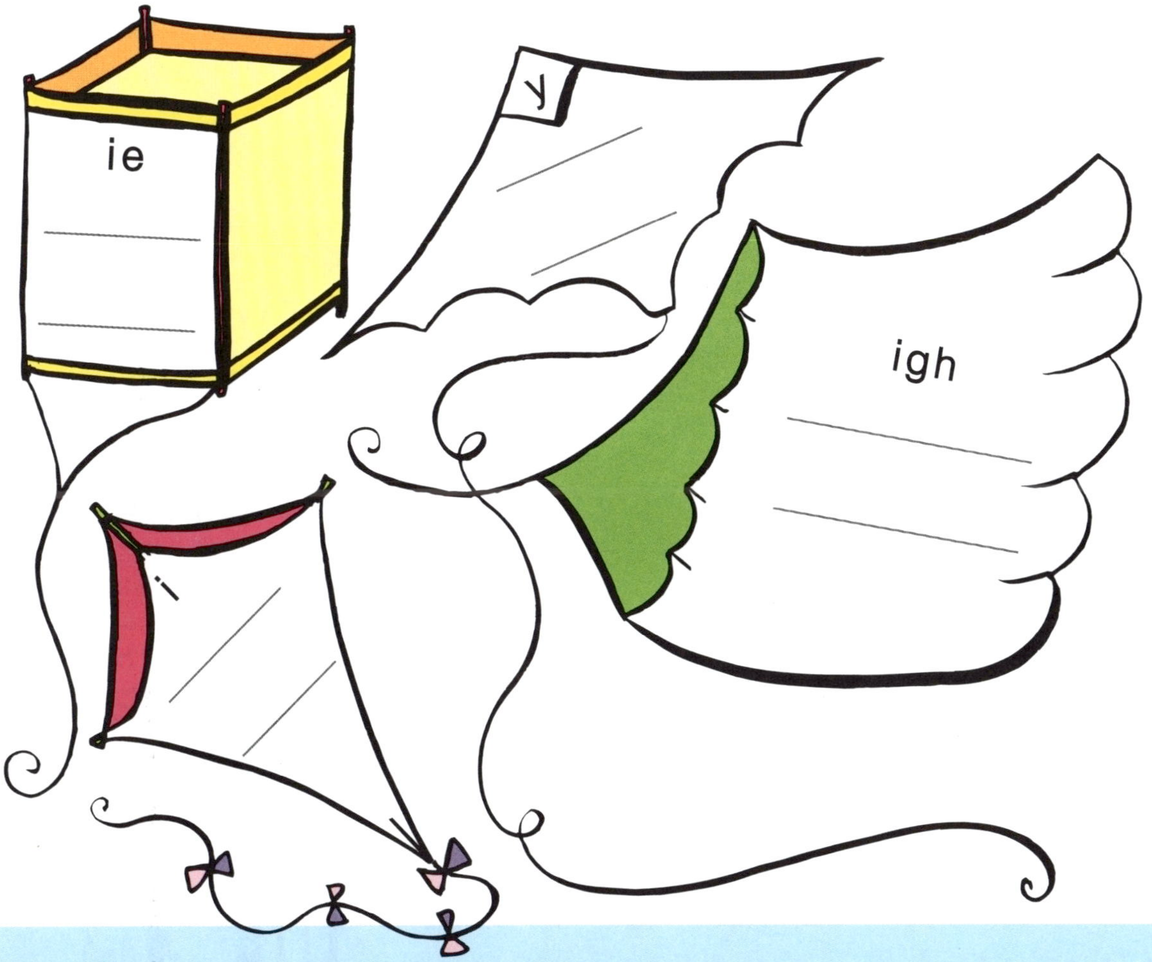

Put a word with a long i sound in each space.

1. She _ _ _ _ _ as hard as she could and eventually managed.

2. To spell correctly, you need to w_ _ _ _ the _ _ _ _ _ letters.

3. _ _ handwriting is qu_ _ _ l_ _ _ yours.

Words that sound the same

To learn to spell words that sound the same but have different meanings.

Sometimes two words sound the same but have different meanings. Often they are spelt differently, too.

Finish these sentences by choosing the correct words from the list.

meat meet bean been

weak week

1. Vegetarians don't eat m_ _ _.

2. M_ _ _ me at the gate.

3. Vegetarians eat lots of b_ _ _s.

4. I have b_ _ _ waiting for hours.

5. My leg was w_ _ _ after I took the bandage off.

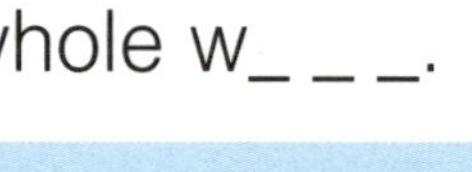

6. My leg hurt for a whole w_ _ _.

To learn to spell more words that sound the same.

More words that sound the same

We call words that sound the same **homophones**.
Here are some more for you to learn.

waste — If we recycle waste paper then it isn't completely wasted.
waist — You wear a belt round your waist.

hare — A hare is like a rabbit, but has longer legs and ears.
hair — Her new haircut suited her.

bare — On a hot day, the sun might burn your bare skin.

bear — I cannot bear seeing that bear made to dance.

The answers to this crossword are words you have learnt.

Across
3. what vegetarians don't eat
6. it's by a beach
7. having no clothes on
8. I'll ______ you after tea.
9. an animal which runs fast
10. Have you ______ to see that film?

Down
1. The skirt was too big for my ______.
2. Rapunzel had long ______.
4. rubbish
5. a polar ______
7. Jack planted one and it grew tall

More prefixes and suffixes

To learn to add **all**, **full** and **til** to words.

Prefixes and suffixes lose a letter when we add them to other words.

all drops an **l** when we use it as a prefix:

altogether **al**though **al**most **al**ways

full and **till** both drop an **l** when we use them as suffixes:

hope**ful** beauti**ful** spoon**ful** un**til**

Something odd happens to **skill** when we add **ful**: skilful

Although I'm **al**most **al**ways **skilful**, today I'm not **al**together hope**ful** of a beauti**ful** result.

Can you make a silly sentence using **ful**, **til** and **al** words?

Humour helps us learn. Encourage your child to make weird and wonderful sentences to practise his or her spellings and vocabulary.

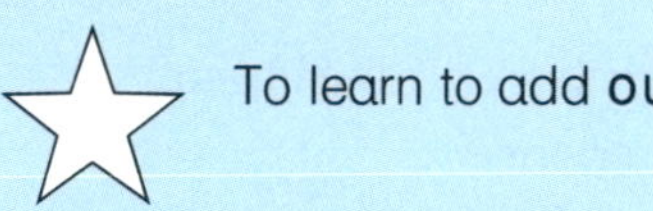

To learn to add **ous** to words.

Words that end in **ous**

Read these words aloud and listen to the endings.

generous famous jealous

Circle the **ous** words in this story:

The zookeeper had to be courageous to pick up the enormous, poisonous snake, as it was famous for being dangerous.

Write each **ous** word below and say what it means.

__________ ______________________________

__________ ______________________________

__________ ______________________________

__________ ______________________________

__________ ______________________________

Choose one of these to learn, using the LOOK SAY method.

LOOK SAY COVER WRITE __________ CHECK

Puzzle practice

☆ To practise what has been learnt so far.

The words for this crossword are all in this book.

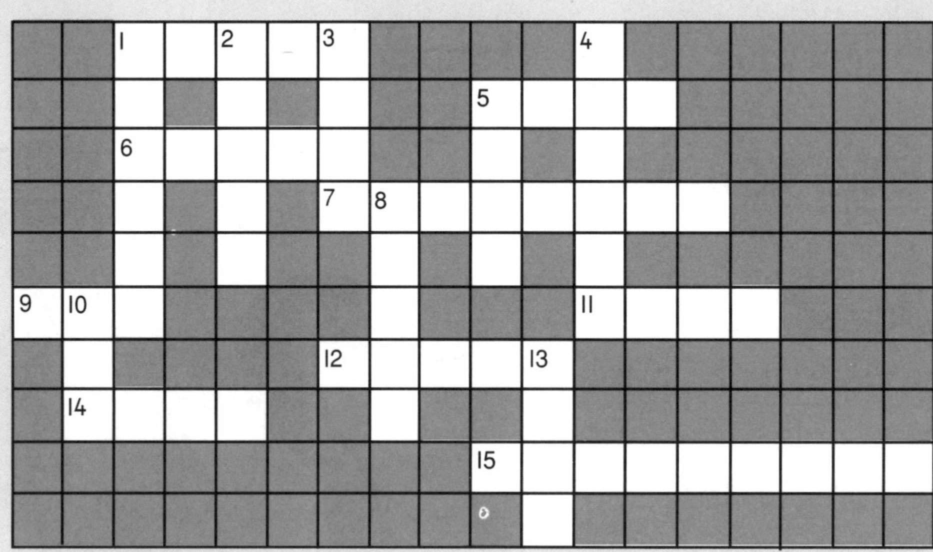

Across

1. use it to tell the time
5. animal that rhymes with hare
6. secretly watched
7. huge
9. opposite of young
11. to leave in water
12. to toss in the air
14. seven days
15. risky

Down

1. rhymes with tasted
2. attempted
3. put in a secret place
4. well known
5. not covered with anything
8. after dark
10. opposite of high
13. not strong

Join the jigsaw pairs to make whole words:

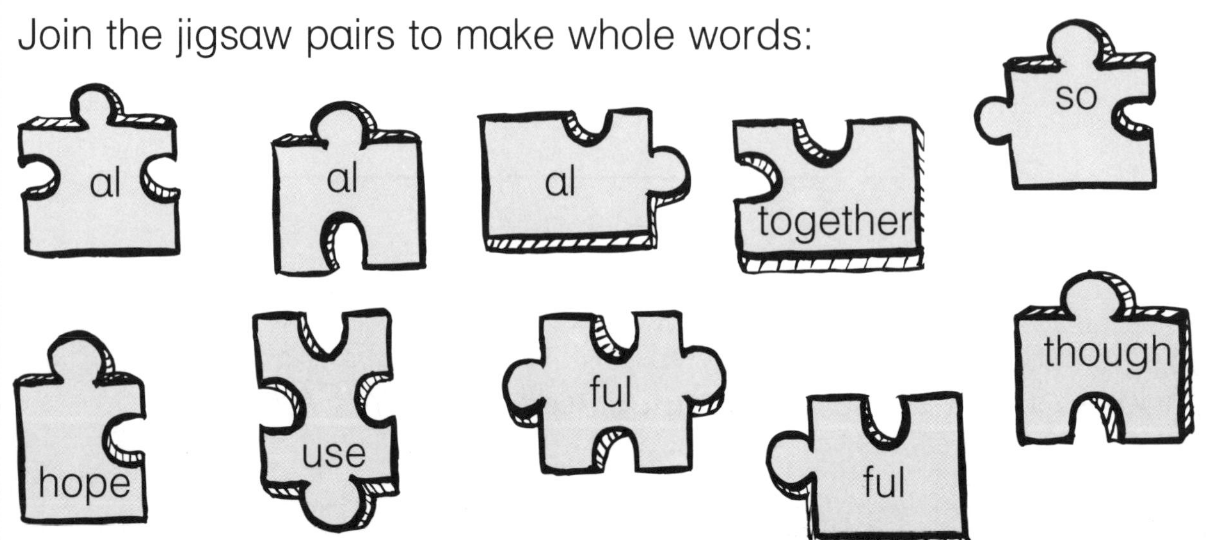

To practise what has been learnt so far.

Puzzle practice

Can you find these words in the wordsearch?

meet	roll
famous	roast
meat	week
hide	weak
throw	hair
fry	know
tyre	float

a	f	r	m	e	a	t	u
f	a	r	e	d	i	h	f
l	m	r	e	x	f	c	e
o	o	o	t	h	r	o	w
a	u	a	y	t	y	r	e
t	s	s	p	r	e	r	e
a	s	t	e	f	i	l	k
a	r	l	l	o	r	a	s
d	e	s	a	r	e	s	h
a	k	n	o	w	e	s	w

The letters of these words are muddled up.
Rearrange them to spell the months of the year.

charM prAil luJy peStbreem broctOe breeDmec

unJraya unJe gutsuA rabuFeyr moveNreb aMy

__________ __________ __________ __________

__________ __________ __________ __________

__________ __________ __________ __________

Get your child to exaggerate the bits of words which cause problems. This will help him or her to remember the correct spelling.

Different beginnings

To learn to add **de** and **di** to words.

Sort these useful words into the right letterboxes.

de	di
________	________
________	________
________	________
________	________

decide
describe
distant
delight
disappeared
despair
different
difficult

Choose two words and use each one in an interesting sentence.

1. ____________________

2. ____________________

Some of the above words have become muddled.
Can you sort them out?

fudfilcti	ripdsae	tnereffid
________	________	________
gedihlt	ppeeaaddrsi	tsiandt
________	________	________

Interesting words

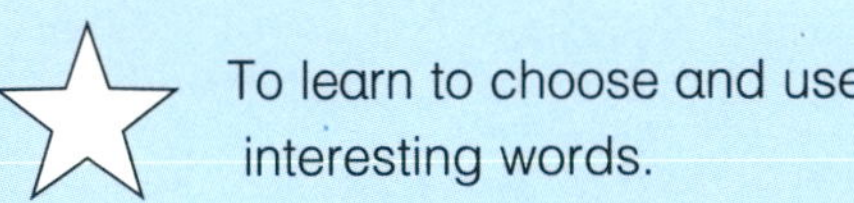

Writing well means using wonderful words.

Choose two of these words and make an interesting sentence with each one.

1. ______________________________

2. ______________________________

Can you fit each word into this crossword?

Interesting adverbs

To learn how to spell adverbs.

Adverbs are **words that describe verbs** (doing words).

I walked **slowly** towards the dog which was still barking **loudly.**

Fill the spaces with the best adverb from the list.

angrily roughly nervously
dangerously wearily awkwardly

After walking eight miles, I sank ________ into a soft armchair.

We approached the barking dog __________.

I heard you shouting ________ at your friends.

The boy was standing _____________ near the edge of the cliff.

She pushed him ________ aside.

After my accident, I walked ___________for months.

Interesting verbs

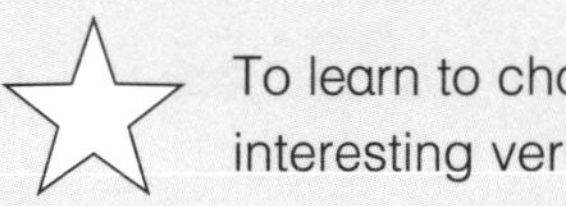

To learn to choose and use interesting verbs.

Another way to write well is to choose interesting verbs.

Here are some examples. Some are other words for **walk** and some are ways of saying **sit**. Sort them into two lists.

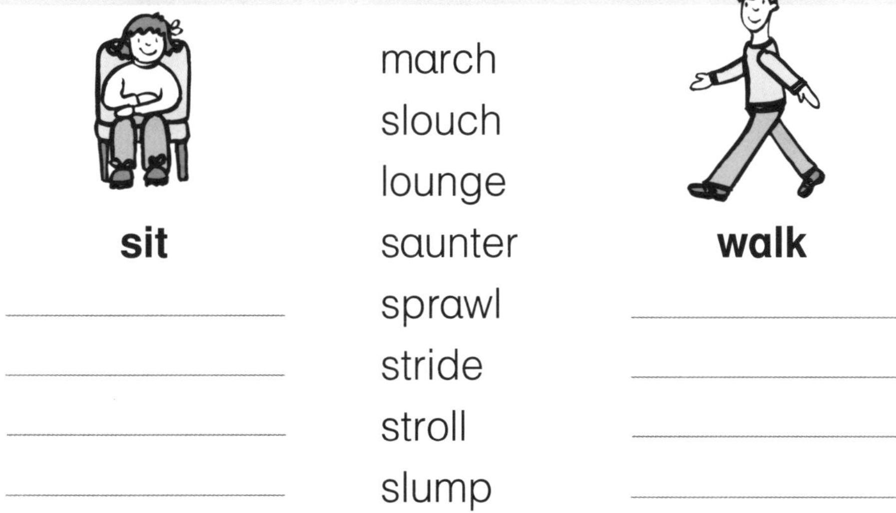

sit		**walk**
	march	
	slouch	
	lounge	
	saunter	
______	sprawl	______
______	stride	______
______	stroll	______
______	slump	______

All these verbs except one are in this wordsearch.

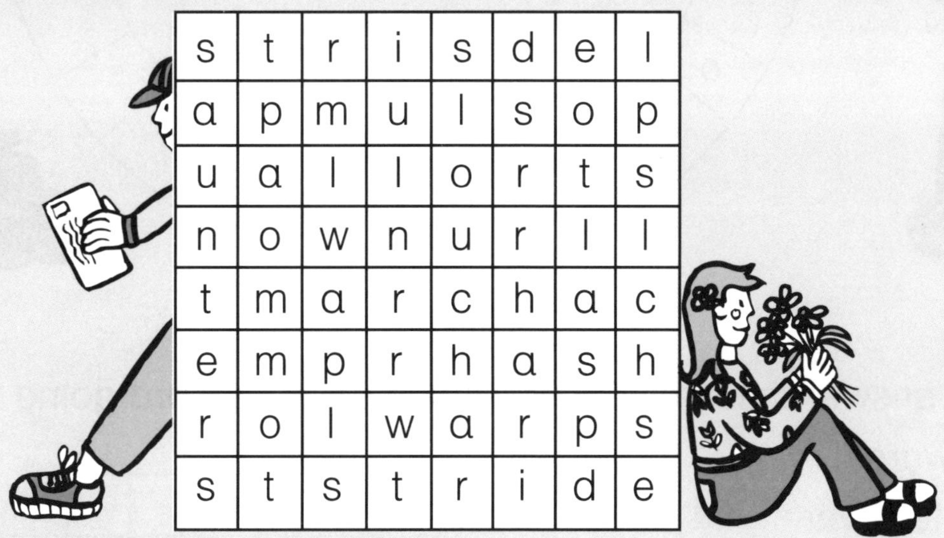

s	t	r	i	s	d	e	l
a	p	m	u	l	s	o	p
u	a	l	l	o	r	t	s
n	o	w	n	u	r	l	l
t	m	a	r	c	h	a	c
e	m	p	r	h	a	s	h
r	o	l	w	a	r	p	s
s	t	s	t	r	i	d	e

Which is the missing verb? ______

If your child has a problem with a particular word, make a decorated picture of it. Pin this to his or her wall and keep returning to it. Soon the spelling will be easy.

Puzzle practice

To practise what has been learnt so far.

You have met all the words for these puzzles.
You can look back to the right page if you need to.

The last letter of each word in the wheel is the first letter of the next word.

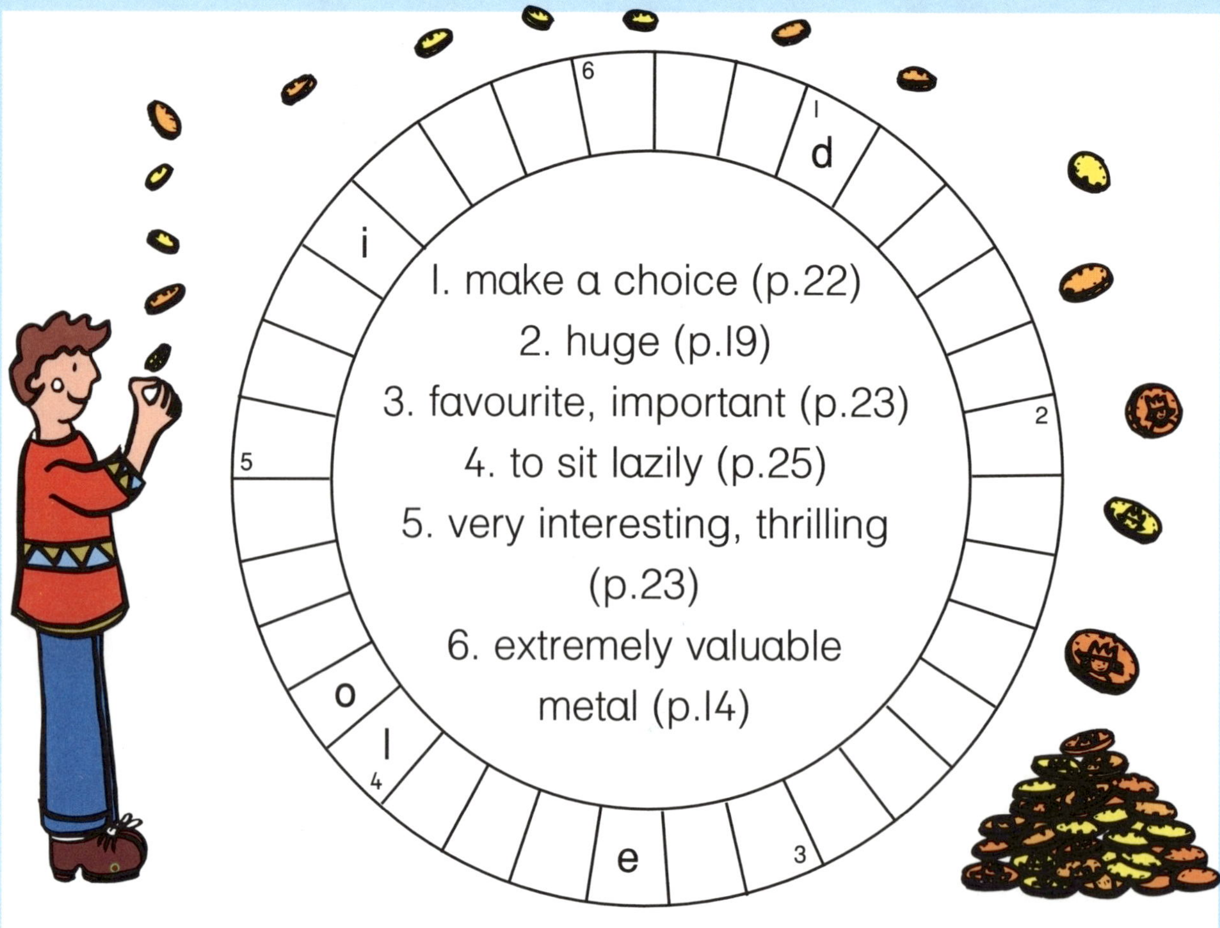

If you answer these clues, you'll see another word going downwards:

1. for ever
2. even though
3. nearly
4. completely

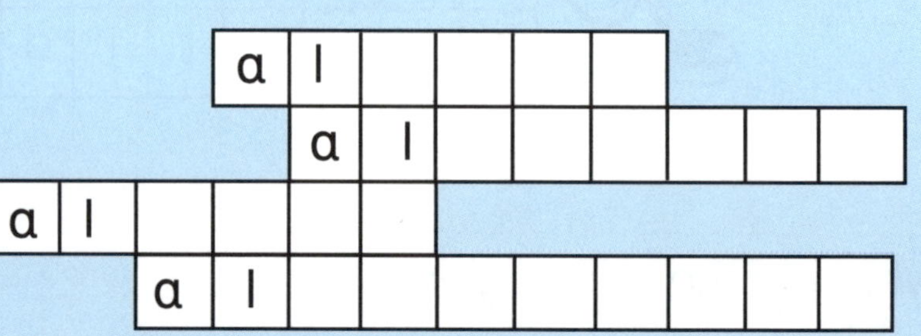

Encourage your child to take pride in the words he or she has already learnt, rather than concentrating on a long list of problem ones.

Puzzle practice

To practise what has been learnt so far.

Answer the clues and fill in the steps.
What do you notice about the first and last words?

1. to cook a piece of meat in an oven (p. 14)
2. to hurl into the air (p. 14)
3. something you need to spell (p. 11)
4. it might hurt you (p. 19)
5. to walk in a relaxed way (p. 25)
6. the opposite of dark and heavy (p. 15)
7. cooked bread (p. 14)

1. a funny story (p. 14)
2. the side of something (p. 5)
3. interesting, thrilling (p. 23)
4. kind, giving (p. 19)
5. frozen rain (p. 14)
6. puts words on paper (p. 15)
7. leave in water (p. 14)

Word puzzles develop lateral thinking and word recall skills as well as spelling. Encourage your child to do the easy bits first and then make sensible guesses which can be changed later.

Starting apostrophes

To learn to use apostrophes for abbreviation.

We write an **apostrophe** when part of a word is missed out.

is not = isn't (the **o** is missed out)

The long words are in the trousers and the shorter words are in the shorts. Cross out the letters in the trousers which are missing in the shorts.

Here are some special ones.

Only write **it's** when it means **it is** or **it has**.

It's time for the dog to have **its** food.

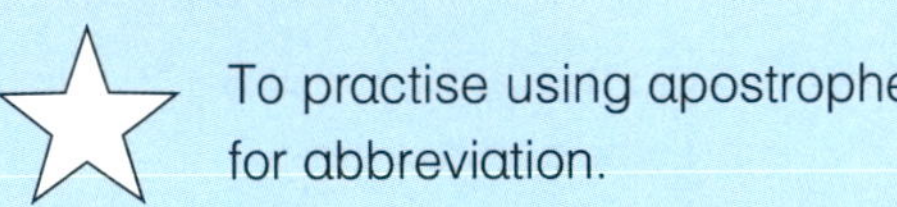
To practise using apostrophes for abbreviation.

Practising apostrophes

Write the shorter version of the words in each space. Remember to put the apostrophe exactly where the missing letters were.

1. King Canute ______ (did not) manage to make the waves go back.

2. I ______ (was not) late today!

3. The Vikings ______ (are not) famous for being gentle.

4. I think ____ (it is) dinner time.

5. I _________ (would not) like to have have lived 300 years ago.

Make up your own sentences with these words:

can't (cannot) ______________________________

there's (there is) ______________________________

they're (they are) ______________________________

who's (who is) ______________________________

Your child may still occasionally put the apostrophe in the wrong place – remind him or her each time. It is important that you make sure he or she understands why it goes where it does.

Using **ie** or **ei**

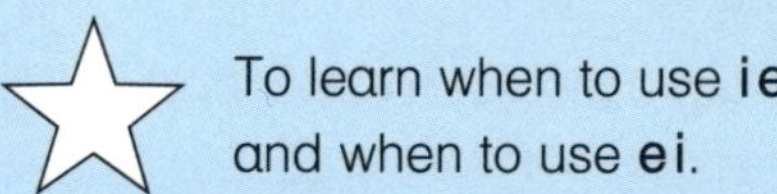

To learn when to use **ie** and when to use **ei**.

The rule is: 'i before **e**, except after **c**', when the sound is 'eee'.

ie
piece
brief
chief
thief
believe
shield

ei
ceiling
receive
deceit
conceited

This word is different. You need to learn it.

seize

If the sound is not 'eee', there's no rule – you just have to learn the words!

eight foreign friend neighbour height weird spied

My w**ei**rd n**ei**ghbour
went to a for**ei**gn country
with a sun umbrella
eight feet in h**ei**ght.

Finding mistakes

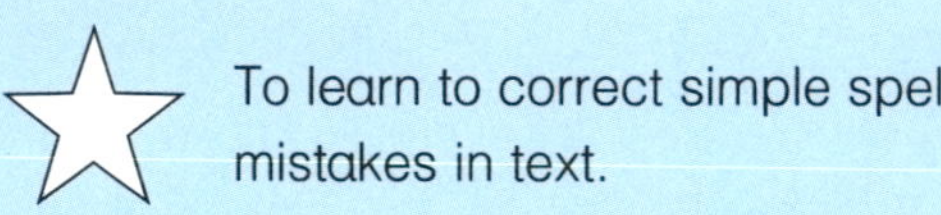

To learn to correct simple spelling mistakes in text.

When we write something, we need to check it carefully. Can you help Sam to check his story before he gives it to Miss Hope? Look out for spelling mistakes, missing words and words in the wrong order.

My Frightening Day

One day last summer, we dicided to go for a walk. Allthough was I soon hungry, my mum said we could'nt eat our picnic yet. I could hardly bare the heat. I moned at my mum and dad untill they said we could stop. I was releived and especially dilighted when I saw the luntch.

I slumped down on the beautifull worm grass, gulping cool orandge juice. Suddenly I spied something – a snake, waching me. My heart thumping as I stared at it. My mouth was dry and my neck prickeld. Was it dangerus? I didn't know if was poisonous. Suddenly it slithered away and dissappeared. No one beleived that I had seen it, but my thudding heart told me I had.

How many mistakes did you find? There are twenty, but if you found fifteen or more you did very well.

Always remind your child to check his or her work and let him or her see you do the same when you write something!

Dictionary page

although
animal
anybody
astronaut
bare
beach
bear
believe
bicycle
bone
bowl
calendar
caravan
catapult
conceited
crocodile
dangerous
decided
delicious
delighted

disappear
double
exciting
enough
frying-pan
happy
hope
hospital
joke
kite
light
love
lunch
marry
mayor
misread
mistake
misunderstanding
octopus
paint
parachute

photograph
quite
rainbow
recorder
silly
snow
spaceship
submarine
subsoil
subway
sunglasses
tail
telephone
telephoto
telescope
television
thunder
toast
trumpet
umbrella
until
use
wheelbarrow

Use this space to write other words you want to remember. They could be words you sometimes forget or just words that you like.